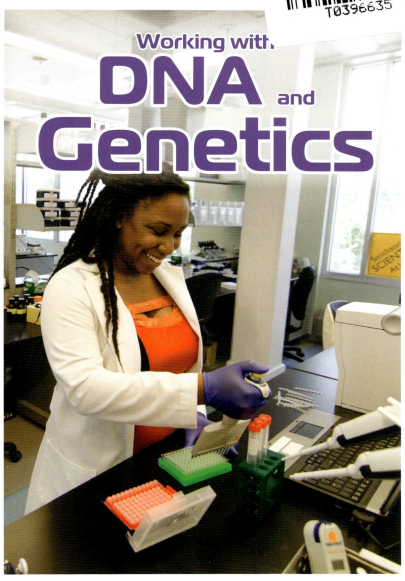

Working with DNA and Genetics

Eric Braun, M.F.A.

Consultants

Robert C. Fleischer
Senior Scientist and Center Head
Smithsonian Conservation Biology Institute's
Center for Conservation Genomics

Cheryl Lane, M.Ed.
Seventh Grade Science Teacher
Chino Valley Unified School District

Michelle Wertman, M.S.Ed.
Literacy Specialist
New York City Public Schools

Publishing Credits

Rachelle Cracchiolo, M.S.Ed., *Publisher*
Emily R. Smith, M.A.Ed., *SVP of Content Development*
Véronique Bos, *VP of Creative*
Dani Neiley, *Editor*
Robin Erickson, *Senior Art Director*
Kevin Pham, *Senior Graphic Designer*

Smithsonian Enterprises

Avery Naughton, *Licensing Coordinator*
Paige Towler, *Editorial Lead*
Jill Corcoran, *Senior Director, Licensed Publishing*
Brigid Ferraro, *Vice President of New Business and Licensing*
Carol LeBlanc, *President*

Image Credits: p.13 AFP via Getty Images; p.14 Alamy Stock Photo; p.19 PETER MENZEL/Science Source; p.23 Millard H. Sharp/Science Source; p.25 South China Morning Post via Getty Images; p.26 QA International/Science Source; all other images from iStock and/or Shutterstock.

Library of Congress Cataloging in Publication Control Number: 2024018895

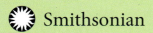

5482 Argosy Avenue
Huntington Beach, CA 92649
www.tcmpub.com
ISBN 979-8-7659-6863-5
© 2025 Teacher Created Materials, Inc.
Printed by: 51497
Printed in : China

© 2025 Smithsonian Institution. The name "Smithsonian" and the Smithsonian logo are registered trademarks owned by the Smithsonian Institution.

This book may not be reproduced or distributed in any way without prior written consent from the publisher.

Table of Contents

Unlocking the Past. 4

Instructions for Life 6

Ancient Secrets 12

Once Upon a Time 18

Return to Dino Days?. 22

The Past Informs the Present 26

STEAM Challenge 28

Glossary. 30

Index. 31

Career Advice 32

Unlocking the Past

Studying the ancient past can be a difficult task. Scientists look at clues in the modern world to learn what they can. They study **artifacts**, such as tools and jewelry, that ancient humans once used. They examine fossils to piece together the skeletons of **extinct** animals. All over the world, scientists examine these items and learn how early humans and animals lived. But many questions remain. Which people used these items? What did these people and animals look like? Why did these animals become extinct?

The answers to these questions can be found in an itty-bitty **molecule** called DNA, short for deoxyribonucleic acid. All organisms are made up of cells that have DNA. That includes humans, moths, blades of grass, and even bacteria! DNA was first discovered in 1869, and scientists have been studying it in-depth since the mid-1900s. Working with DNA is a delicate and careful process. Special labs and lab equipment help scientists complete this complex job. In recent years, scientists have also developed new methods for studying ancient DNA. This has allowed them to gain insight into how humans and animals lived and **evolved**.

dinosaur skeletons at the Natural History Museum in Los Angeles, California

DNA might be microscopic, but the amount of information scientists gain from it is enormous. Let's take a closer look at DNA and how it changes over time, as well as **genetics**. And let's explore some questions of our own, including whether DNA could bring dinosaurs back to life!

Scientists use a variety of technology to study delicate strands of DNA.

Instructions for Life

Although you can't see it with the naked eye, DNA is everywhere. It exists inside the nucleus of every living cell. DNA is found in chromosomes, which are threadlike structures in a cell's nucleus. Some DNA also exists in mitochondria, the oval-shaped structures in a cell. DNA forms a spiral, ladderlike structure that is called a *double helix*. DNA is made up of four chemicals called *bases* that pair together and repeat in different orders. Together, these chemicals form a code that contains a large amount of information. DNA has all the details an organism needs to develop, function, grow, and reproduce. This means that DNA molecules are kind of like instructions, or blueprints, for life.

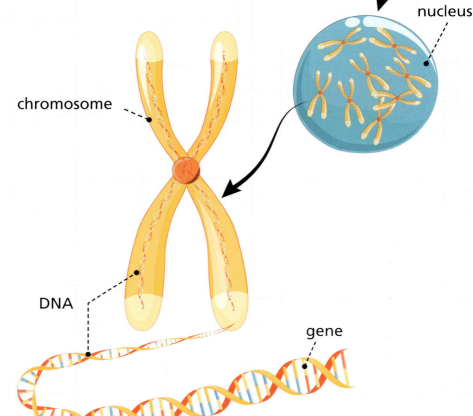

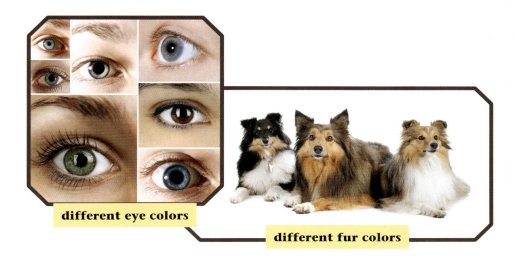

different eye colors

different fur colors

Chromosomes have segments of DNA bases called *genes*. Genes carry information about the physical and behavioral characteristics of an organism. These characteristics are also called *traits*. In humans, traits can include eye color, skin tone, and height. In animals, traits can include skin or fur texture, eye shape, and body color. Plants have traits, too! Height, stem width, and leaf size are some plant traits. DNA holds all this information in one place.

All the DNA inside a person's cells makes up the human genome. This is all the genetic information that makes up a human. The genome is like an instruction manual, keeping everything in order.

A Small Percentage

The human genome has about 25,000 genes that are arranged in the same order. About 99.9 percent of everyone's genome is the same. The remaining 0.1 percent is where all the differences among people come from. Our genes in that 0.1 percent are what make us unique!

Heredity

In families, each **generation** contains some of the same DNA as the previous one. Through **reproduction**, DNA is passed from a parent organism to its **offspring**. This is called *heredity*. In humans, only a portion of DNA gets passed down. If all of it were passed down, everyone would have the same exact traits. Everyone would look and act the same.

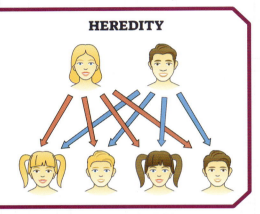

HEREDITY

Every human baby gets half of their genes from one parent and half from the other parent. Because they share some genes, children typically look like their biological parents or siblings. However, this is not always the case. That's because the copy of each gene that gets passed from the parent to the child is random. So, each child has a unique combination of genes, meaning they have a unique set of traits, too. This is why two siblings in the same family might have different colored hair or eyes. The only exception to this rule is identical twins. Identical twins share the same genes.

DNA Over Time

As DNA is passed down over time, it can change. First, when organisms reproduce, their genes become mixed in their offspring. This mixing leads to genetic **variation** over generations. This is why a child might look very different from their biological great-grandparents. Next are **mutations**. These are mistakes or natural changes to the DNA itself, and they happen rarely. Most mutations are not noticeable. But some of them can cause health problems, such as cancer or other diseases. Last, some changes in DNA create **variants** in traits that make it more likely for a species to survive in its environment. These helpful variations are called *adaptations*. When they are passed down over many generations, adaptations may spread and become a trait for the species.

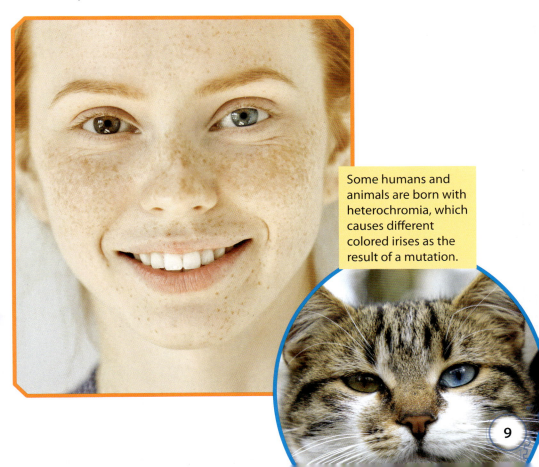

Some humans and animals are born with heterochromia, which causes different colored irises as the result of a mutation.

Working with DNA

Did you know that about 10,000 human cells can fit on the head of a pin? Now, picture having to work with just *one* of those cells—and the even smaller DNA that is inside. Scientists have a tough job ahead of them when they study DNA, and here's how they do it.

Scientists first find a source of DNA from an organism. DNA can be found in cells, so they might use body tissue, such as blood. DNA can also be found in saliva, which is used for most DNA tests. For ancient DNA, scientists usually work with bones.

Isolating the strands of DNA comes next. This involves pulling the DNA out of a cell so scientists can work with it. First, DNA has to come off of a chromosome. Then, it goes through the globe-shaped nucleus and travels through the tough cell wall. This all needs to be done carefully so that the DNA is not damaged. Depending on the source, different extraction methods are used. But typically, scientists use certain types of enzymes. These are special liquids that can break down the barriers of cell structures.

When DNA has been extracted, scientists can study it. They examine the strands and can read, or decode, the information it holds. They can also store the DNA in special containers for later use or study.

Special machines called *sequencers* help scientists study DNA.

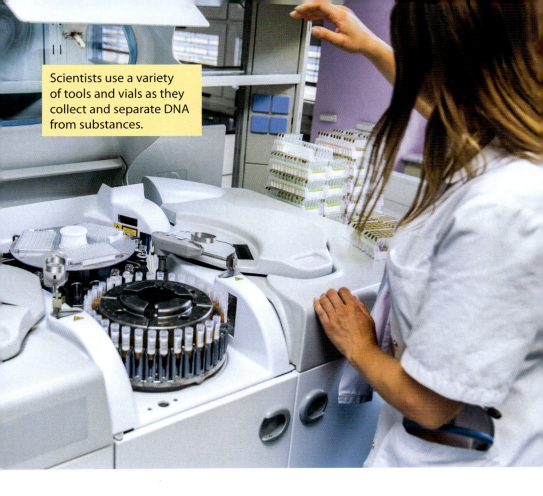

Scientists use a variety of tools and vials as they collect and separate DNA from substances.

SCIENCE

Center for Conservation Genomics

At this lab, scientists study DNA for many reasons. They study animal DNA to learn about genetic variation in species. They learn how animals evolved and adapted over time. This information can be used to determine methods of **conservation**. Scientists at this lab also study ancient DNA.

Ancient Secrets

Imagine that you could see a photo of one of your ancestors from thousands of years ago. Maybe you would notice some physical similarities to yourself or your family members, such as hair color. But you would also see some big differences. Maybe the person would be much shorter than you. And if you could somehow see inside their cells, you could learn even more from their DNA. You could learn about all their traits, not just the physical ones. You would also learn how those traits have changed over many generations.

By studying ancient DNA, scientists can learn more than ever before about ancient populations. Ancient DNA is like a time capsule that provides a view into history. Scientists can use ancient DNA to learn new information about plants, animals, and humans that lived long ago. Scientists can learn how they lived and evolved. Plus, they can gain new insights into how evolution shaped modern-day organisms.

Scientists have tried to extract DNA from insects in amber, but they have not been successful yet.

Scientists performed DNA testing on pieces of ancient manuscripts called the *Dead Sea Scrolls*. DNA tests helped scientists learn more about the origins of these texts.

Ancient DNA is even more delicate to work with than modern DNA. Due to its age, it can be hard to extract without damaging it. But although it is a tough process for scientists, their findings with ancient DNA have unlocked new information about the past.

FUN FACT

Scientists have found ancient DNA in a variety of places. They have found it in fossils, extinct animal pelts, and soil samples. Scientists have extracted DNA from museum specimens and artifacts. They have even found DNA in mummies!

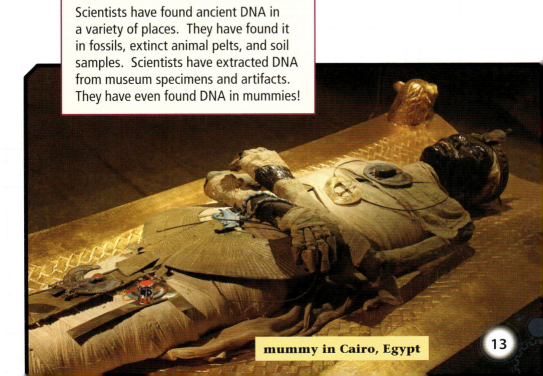

mummy in Cairo, Egypt

Consider the Quagga

A breakthrough moment in DNA studies occurred in 1984. That year marked the first time scientists examined the DNA of an extinct species. This species is called the *quagga*. These animals were hunted to extinction in southern Africa in the late 1800s. They looked like a cross between horses and zebras, and the front parts of their bodies had stripes.

Quagga DNA provided surprising information. Scientists were able to take a sample of quagga tissue from a pelt in a museum. They used the cells in the tissue to examine the DNA. During their examination, scientists found that quaggas were more closely related to zebras than horses. They discovered this by comparing quagga DNA with horse and zebra DNA. And over time, as technology improved, scientists discovered even more. They now know that quaggas are a subspecies of the plains zebra. They are not a separate species, like they had originally thought.

Since this first study, scientists have read the DNA of thousands of ancient organisms. They've studied the DNA of crops from thousands of years ago. They've studied animals from the last ice age. They've even studied **Neanderthals**. And as technology improves even more, scientists will be able to study a wider range of organisms.

Woolly rhinos lived during the last ice age.

Neanderthal

FUN FACT

In 2014, scientists examined DNA from a Neanderthal. This person lived tens of thousands of years ago in Siberia. Scientists found that 99.7 percent of Neanderthal DNA is identical to that of modern humans!

DNA and Diversity

Scientists have examined DNA to see the genetic **diversity** in a species. This refers to slight differences in DNA within a species. For example, certain animals might have different traits than others. Different traits apply to food, too. Just think of how many kinds of tomatoes there are! These differences can allow a species to adapt to their changing environment. This adaptation gives them a higher chance of survival. By studying this, scientists have learned why some species change over time.

Peppered moths show an example of this change. Before the mid-1700s, these moths mostly had light-colored wings. They could use **camouflage** to blend in against white tree trunks for safety. But then, the Industrial Revolution occurred. Air pollution killed light-colored **lichens** on tree bark, which made tree trunks appear darker. The moths no longer blended in with the bark. They became easier prey for birds. However, peppered moths didn't die off. Some of them began to develop dark wings so they could hide against the trees. Dark-winged moths were more likely to survive. This color-changing adaptation helped the species survive even when their environment changed. In 2016, scientists were able to examine the DNA of peppered moths and find the exact mutation that caused this change in color.

Using DNA in this way allows scientists to understand adaptation more clearly. They can also study when these changes occurred within a species.

white peppered moth

Darker peppered moths have an easier time blending in with their surroundings.

Once Upon a Time

It is fairly easy to extract DNA from modern subjects. That's because people's DNA gets all over the things they touch. For example, imagine that a scientist brought your T-shirt to a lab. Your fingerprints and skin cells are all over it, so they could easily get your DNA from it.

But when it comes to ancient artifacts, it's a whole different story. Extracting ancient DNA from a tool or piece of jewelry is much harder because DNA degrades over time. After thousands of years, only fragments, or parts, of DNA may exist. Sometimes, no DNA from an artifact can be found at all.

Until recently, the only way to retrieve DNA from ancient humans was through well-preserved remains. Bones and teeth were the best sources because of their hardness. These remains could stand the test of time. To retrieve DNA from these samples, scientists ground up the bone to make a powder that they could analyze. They had to be very careful to avoid infecting the samples with modern DNA.

Genetic Engineering

Scientists can read DNA. But did you know that they can also alter it? Genetic engineering involves deleting, adding, or altering parts of DNA. Special technology is needed to do this. Scientists can apply these techniques to create new crops and medicines.

Corn has been genetically modified to be resistant to pests.

As technology has advanced, sampling tools have improved. Scientists can now retrieve DNA samples from a wider range of remains and areas around the world. And the more samples scientists can find and analyze, the clearer picture they can get of how people and animals evolved, where they came from, and how they lived.

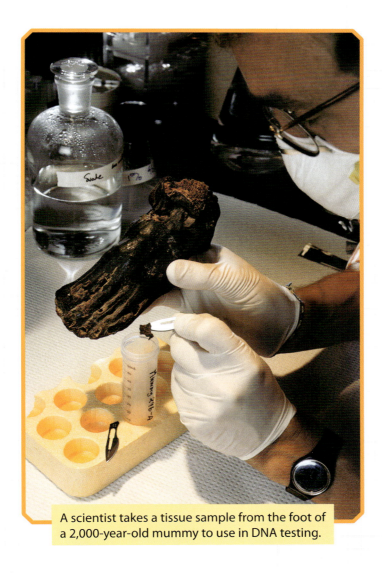

A scientist takes a tissue sample from the foot of a 2,000-year-old mummy to use in DNA testing.

The Tooth and the Girl

For many years, scientists in Germany tried to remove DNA from ancient artifacts without cutting or damaging them. In 2019, they were successful. An archaeologist gave the scientists a 20,000-year-old elk tooth found in a cave in Siberia. The tooth was caked in dirt, but scientists could see it had a hole drilled through it. Clearly, it had been worn as jewelry. The scientists began to wonder about the person who wore it. What was their life like? Was the tooth passed down through generations?

Siberian elk

This tooth was a good candidate for DNA testing. That's because the archaeologists who found it were wearing masks, gloves, and coveralls. These protections helped prevent the tooth from being contaminated by modern DNA. Also, the surface of a tooth is porous. This means that the ancient elk tooth may have trapped skin cells or sweat from the person who wore it.

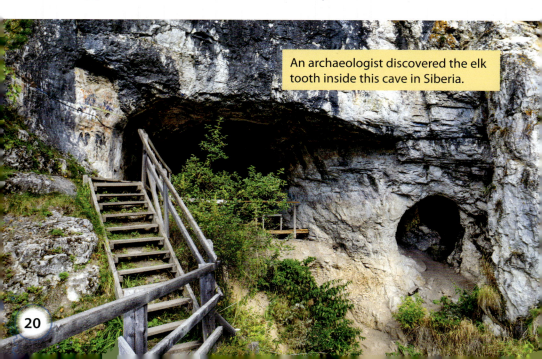
An archaeologist discovered the elk tooth inside this cave in Siberia.

Scientists use gloves and clothing protection in sterile labs.

The German scientists tested the tooth in their **sterile** lab. Thanks to the method they had developed over the years, the test was a success! They found two types of DNA: elk and female human. After further studies, scientists discovered even more. They found that the woman lived with a group of people about 1,931 kilometers (1,200 miles) away from where the tooth was found. Since she was a long way from home, scientists think she could have been traveling to trade with other groups.

This technique for extracting DNA will be valuable for learning more about the ancient past. Scientists think it could shed light on how prehistoric people lived.

TECHNOLOGY

Archaeological Washing Machine

Elena Essel, the lead scientist on the study of the ancient elk tooth, compared their method to "a washing machine for ancient artifacts." First, the scientists put the tooth into a chemical solution in a machine. Then, they slowly heated it to about 90 °C (194 °F). DNA began to emerge, leaving the tooth unharmed.

Return to Dino Days?

Perhaps you have seen movies where dinosaurs are brought back from extinction. In these fictional plots, scientists use the DNA of these long-dead creatures to bring them to life again. Imagine what it would be like if you saw a T-rex hunting for meat outside your home. Hey, *you* are meat, aren't you? Better stay inside!

Because scientists can access ancient DNA, you might be wondering if this could happen in real life. But bringing dinosaurs back to life is not possible. The technology that this would require does not exist. It would be impossible to re-create the exact same species that lived long ago. Plus, whole strands of DNA cannot survive for millions of years. The last dinosaurs on Earth died about 66 million years ago. Scientists know that only fragments of DNA could survive for that long.

However, scientists still look for evidence of cells in dinosaur fossils. Some scientists in the United States and China studied the embryo of a baby hadrosaur. They analyzed the tissues inside the skull and found evidence of **cartilage** cells. This was the first time that cartilage cells had been isolated from a fossil. Further testing showed that some proteins and chromosomes were preserved inside these cells. Scientists are still trying to confirm whether these cells contain fragments of DNA. But even if they do, the quality of the DNA will likely be too degraded to read. Still, this finding is significant. It gives new hope to the idea that well-preserved cells may be found.

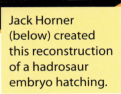

Jack Horner (below) created this reconstruction of a hadrosaur embryo hatching.

Jurassic Park

In the *Jurassic Park* movies, scientists bring dinosaurs back to life. A **paleontologist** named Jack Horner was an advisor to these movies. And in 2011, Horner tried to re-create dinosaurs! He worked with scientists to rewrite the DNA of chickens. His team worked to modify the genes in chicken embryos. But in the end, they were not able to create dinosaurs.

Mammoth Mysteries

While seeing dinosaurs come back to life is out of the question, what about other extinct animals? Again, it is not very likely. Scientists may not be able to get all their DNA. Even if they did, it only provides information. Using it to exactly re-create an extinct animal is impossible. Still, working with the DNA of extinct animals can create exciting possibilities.

The DNA of woolly mammoths has been studied for many years. These were fuzzy elephant-like creatures with massive tusks. Most of them became extinct about 10,000 years ago. These creatures mostly lived on the tundra. Many woolly mammoth fossils have been found in the frozen soil of Siberia. This is the same place where the elk tooth pendant was found. The **permafrost** provides a good environment for preservation. And some of the woolly mammoth fossils are preserved well enough to contain readable DNA.

Scientists estimate that woolly mammoths were 3–3.7 meters (10–12 feet) tall.

The body of this baby mammoth was preserved for 40,000 years in the permafrost of Siberia.

This is where genetic engineering comes in. Scientists examined the genes of woolly mammoths. They found that elephant genes are very similar. Some people have wondered what would happen if you could combine their DNA. Would you end up with a re-creation of a woolly mammoth? The new animal might look like a woolly mammoth and even behave like one, but it would not be a true woolly mammoth. Its genes and DNA would be different.

FUN FACT

Cloning means creating an identical copy of something. Clones share the same DNA. Scientists have been able to clone some mammals over the past few decades. They first take the nucleus from one of the cells of an existing animal. Then, they put it into the egg cell of another animal so it can develop. Scientists are still working on their methods for this difficult process.

The Past Informs the Present

Earth was formed about 4.5 billion years ago. The first life forms on Earth were microscopic organisms. They came into existence between 3.8 and 3.5 billion years ago. Since then, life on Earth has gotten much more complex. First, there were multicellular plants. Then, around 800 million years ago, the first animals—sponges—existed. Dinosaurs lived between about 245 and 66 million years ago. Finally, modern humans appeared about 315,000 years ago.

Considering how old our planet is, people haven't been around for very long. But we can still learn what the world was like long ago, thanks to ancient remains. While no humans have ever seen a live dinosaur, fossils can tell us about their existence. Scientists can study bones and teeth to see fragments of once-living cells. They can examine museum specimens to extract DNA from hundred-year-old tissues. And because of recent advances in technology, they can sometimes pull DNA from old artifacts.

Being able to read DNA from extinct animals and ancient times gives us a window into our history. We can learn about events that affected ancient life. We can see when adaptations occurred in animal species. And we can discover more about how people and animals once lived.

Thanks to fossils and DNA, scientists know what species have lived in the oceans and on land over billions of years.

STEAM CHALLENGE

Define the Problem

When paleontologists discover an ancient item at a site, they have to transport the item without damaging or contaminating it. They must be able to take the item from the site to a lab where they can study it and extract DNA from the specimen. Your task is to design and create a closed container that paleontologists can use to hold and transport ancient artifacts from a site to the lab without contaminating the specimen.

Constraints: You may only use the materials provided to you. The container must protect the artifact from damage and contamination.

Criteria: Your container must hold an artifact in place without moving when carried. The model must include an opening to place the artifact inside, and you must be able to see the artifact inside.

Research and Brainstorm

Where do paleontologists conduct their work? What types of artifacts and specimens do paleontologists find on site?

Design and Build

Sketch two or more designs for your container. Label the parts and the materials. Choose the design you think will work best. Then, build your container.

Test and Improve

Share your model with others. Demonstrate how the model works by placing the artifact in the container. Carry the artifact across the room in the container. Was the container successful at holding the artifact in place? How can you improve it? Can you modify your design to allow space for more than one artifact? Modify your design and reassess how well it meets the criteria.

Reflect and Share

What about this challenge did you find most interesting? What problems did you encounter and how did you resolve them? What other types of materials could you use for your model?

Glossary

artifacts—objects, such as tools, jewelry, or pottery, made by humans

camouflage—coloration that blends with an environment or surroundings

cartilage—a somewhat flexible, lightweight tissue that gives structural support in skeletons

conservation—planned management of a natural resource or species to prevent exploitation and promote protection

diversity—genetic differences within a species

evolved—(of a species) developed and changed gradually over time

extinct—no longer existing

generation—a group of organisms that makes up a single step in the line of descent from an ancestor

genetics—the study of genes and traits over time

lichens—plantlike organisms growing on rocks or trees

molecule—a microscopic chemical compound made up of two or more atoms bonded together

mutations—changes to the gene structures that result in trait variations

Neanderthals—an extinct species of very early humans

offspring—a baby born from a parent

paleontologist—an expert who studies fossil remains of animals and plants

permafrost—a permanently frozen layer of earth beneath the ground's surface

reproduction—the process of producing offspring

sterile—clean and free from all bacteria and microorganisms

variants—versions of something that are different from other versions of the same thing

variation—the presence of different genes in a species

Index

adaptations, 9, 16, 27
artifacts, 4, 13, 18, 20–21, 26
Center for Conservation Genomics, 11
chromosomes, 6–7, 10, 23
clones, 25
dinosaurs, 4–5, 22–24, 26
DNA extraction, 10–11, 18, 21
elk tooth, 20–21, 24
Essel, Elena, 21
fossils, 4, 13, 23–24, 26
genes, 6–9, 23, 25
genetic diversity, 16
genetic engineering, 18, 25
genetic variation, 9, 11
heredity, 8
Horner, Jack, 23

Industrial Revolution, 16
Jurassic Park, 23
mitochondria, 6
mummies, 13, 19
mutations, 9, 16
Neanderthals, 15
nucleus, 6, 10, 25
peppered moths, 16–17
quagga, 14
reproduction, 6, 8
Siberia, 15, 20, 24–25
traits, 7–9, 12, 16
woolly mammoths, 24–25
zebras, 14

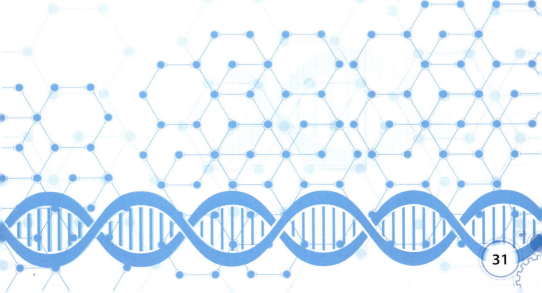

CAREER ADVICE
from Smithsonian

Do you want to study DNA or be a scientist?

Here are some tips to keep in mind for the future.

"Take classes in genetics and molecular biology of course, but don't forget to take classes in evolution and ecology (and mathematics) to analyze and make sense of the genetic data you find."

– *Robert C. Fleischer, Senior Scientist and Center Head, Center for Conservation Genomics*

"See if you can find ways to engage in community service projects with local conservation organizations that connect you with nature, and learn about the importance of being environmentally conscious."

– *Jesús Maldonado, Research Geneticist, Center for Conservation Genomics*